FANTASTIC
FACTS
ABOUT
AUSTRALIA'S
EXTRAORDINARY
ANIMALS
FRANCES PAYNE
AF584438
REDBACK
publishing

Redback Publishing
Suite 6, 13a Narabang Way,
Belrose NSW 2085
Australia

www.redbackpublishing.com
orders@redbackpublishing.com

978-1-922322-71-5

Author: Fances Payne
Editor: Caroline Thomas
Designer: Redback Publishing

Original illustrations © Redback Publishing 2021
Originated by Redback Publishing

Acknowledgements
Abbreviations: l—left, r—right, b—bottom, t—top, c—centre, m—middle
We would like to thank the following for permission to reproduce photographs: (Images © shutterstock), p4t Diprotodon optatum, by Dmitry Bogdanov [CC BY 3.0 (https://creativecommons.org/licenses/by/3.0)], via Wikimedia commons, p19tm Southern brush-tailed rock wallaby, by ACT Government [CC0] https://upload.wikimedia.org/wikipedia/commons/1/1f/Rhonda-emblem.jpg, via Wikimedia commons, p30 Drop Bear illustration, original work courtesy of Caroline Thomas.

Every effort has been made to contact copyright holders of any material reproduced in this book. Any omissions will be rectified in subsequent printings if notice is given to the publisher.

A catalogue record for this book is available from the National Library of Australia

CONTENTS

Fruit bat

Red kangaroo

Red land crab

Curious Ancient Animals

Diprotodon optatum

MEGAFAUNA (Really, really BIG animals!)

There used to be a time when ancient relatives of wombats were as big as horses. Modern echidnas are related to animals that were as big as dogs, and goannas used to be as large and dangerous as modern crocodiles. All of these creatures, as well as many more, are called megafauna, which means big animals.

WHAT CAUSED THE MEGAFAUNA TO DIE OUT?

In Australia, most of the megafauna became extinct between 7,000 and 45,000 years ago due to a combination of climate change and human migration. Since Aboriginal people have lived on the continent of Australia for at least 65,000 years, they would have been familiar with the giant animals and would have hunted them for thousands of years. It is likely that this hunting may have contributed to the megafauna extinction, but animal numbers were also decreasing naturally as the ancient climate warmed.

Aboriginal painting, Kakadu, Northern Territory

LIONS IN AUSTRALIA

Yes, there used to be lions in Australia. They looked a little like the big cats of Africa and Asia do today, but the Australian lion was a marsupial animal, not a placental one like modern tigers, panthers and lions. Marsupial lions lived in Australia for millions of years, and were still around when people first came to the land 65,000 years ago.

30cm

Giant Australian Trilobite fossil (*Selenopeltis*)

Stromatolites

The time machines of the animal world

Q. Where in Australia can you stand by the ocean and imagine you are living on Earth 3.7 billion years ago?

A. In Shark Bay, Western Australia.

Shark Bay

WESTERN AUSTRALIA

Perth

stromatolite

Along the shoreline at Shark Bay there is a very special place called Hamelin Pool, where there are masses of stromatolites, an ancient type of primitive living thing. These tiny creatures form clumps that look like rocks. The ancestors of the stromatolites at Shark Bay were alive long before the first living creatures with legs left the oceans to walk on the land.

Since our Earth is only 4.5 billion years old, the stromatolites have been flourishing for a mind-bendingly long time!

Aussie Dinosaurs

Millions of years ago, long before the megafauna existed, dinosaurs flourished across Australia. Fossils from many locations in Australia have contributed to our knowledge of what life used to be like when dinosaurs were the dominant animals on Earth.

DINOSAURS TAKE A WALK

Along the coast near Broome, in Western Australia, there are preserved footprints of many types of dinosaurs, dating from 120 million years ago.

MINI-DINOSAURS IN A CAGE

Birds are the descendants of dinosaurs. Look at a cockatoo's claws and scaly legs and then imagine them on a dinosaur, metres high! Although not exactly the same, the sharp claws and quick movements of modern birds give us an idea of what a living dinosaur might have been like. Scientists now believe that a large number of dinosaurs even had colourful feathers to keep them warm and for displaying to other dinosaurs.

A FEW OF THE MANY DINOSAURS THAT ONCE LIVED IN AUSTRALIA

AUSTRALOVENATOR

- lived 95 million years ago
- a fast runner and vicious hunter
- 5 metres long

RHOETOSAURUS

- lived 170 million years ago
- ate plants
- 12 metres long

MUTTABURRASAURUS

- lived 100 million years ago
- ate plants
- 7 metres long

DIAMANTINASAURUS

- lived 95 million years ago
- ate plants
- 15 metres long

MYTHUNGA

- flying dinosaur
- lived 100 million years ago
- hunted for fish
- 5 metre wingspan

Precious But Dangerous!

KILLER PLATYPUS?

The male platypus has a venomous spine on its hind leg. Venom is a rarity amongst mammals, and it gives the platypus one more unusual feature to add to all the others it has. The venom can kill a small animal and is very painful to humans. Who would have thought that a furry little platypus could kill?

More Facts About the Amazing Platypus

- When British people first saw a dead platypus that was brought back from Australia, they thought it was a hoax. Surely someone had stitched together parts from different animals to create such an oddity?
- The platypus reproduces by laying eggs, like a bird or a reptile.
- The bill is extremely sensitive and allows the platypus to find its food in the mud at the bottom of streams.
- The platypus is unique. Nothing like it exists anywhere else on Earth.

SPIKY ECHIDNA

The echidna's spines or spikes are not venomous, but they can cause a nasty injury to humans or other animals. Like the platypus, the echidna reproduces by laying eggs. The mother then feeds her babies with milk she produces. A baby echidna is called a 'puggle', and the mother makes it leave her pouch once it starts to grow spines.

IS THE DINGO A DOG?

Dingoes look and behave much like domestic dogs, but they are not the same type of animal. Dogs have been bred by humans for thousands of years as workers and companions, but the dingo is a wild animal. This means it does not see humans as its natural friends. Even when a dingo puppy is raised by humans, it still retains many of its wild behaviours.

Because they are so intelligent, wild dingoes can be dangerous if people feed them or encourage them to come to houses or campsites. Attacks on children and babies have occurred when dingoes lose their fear of being near humans.

HELP! THERE'S A SNAKE IN MY HOUSE!

Aboriginal Australians have shared their environment with poisonous snakes for thousands of years. With the growing construction of farms, houses and cities, the presence of a snake near or inside a building is not uncommon, but can be a very frightening experience. Most Australians do not know what to do when confronted by a snake in their garden or home, and they have to call in an expert snake handler to remove the creature. Australia does have a large number of deadly snakes, so being wary of them is sensible. Australia's native snakes are protected animals. Killing them for no reason is not allowed.

INLAND TAIPAN

Lives in central Australia. It has the most dangerous venom of any land snake in the world. Fortunately, it does not like living near human settlements, and hangs out in remote, rocky regions instead.

RED-BELLIED BLACK SNAKE

Lives on the east coast of Australia and is common around the outer and bushy suburbs of Sydney. This beautiful but dangerous snake will strike if annoyed.

DIAMOND PYTHON

Although huge – growing up to three metres long – diamond pythons do not have venom, although they may bite. They kill their prey by squeezing them to death. The diamond python lives in coastal New South Wales, sometimes crawling around inside roof areas, where they hunt for mice.

DEATH ADDER

Found in eastern and southern Australia. The death adder keeps still rather than fleeing, making it very dangerous if someone treads on it by mistake.

EASTERN BROWN SNAKE

This plain-looking, highly venomous snake is known for being aggressive if cornered. It lives in eastern Australia.

TIGER SNAKE

Named for its black and yellow bands, the tiger snake lives in southeastern Australia.

COPPERHEAD SNAKE

The only local snake that lives in cold regions in eastern Australia.

The Biggest Animals

CASSOWARIES

The cassowary is a large and powerful bird that can be dangerous to humans if it feels threatened. Cassowaries live in rainforests in the warm, northern parts of Australia. As with emus, it is the male bird's role to look after the chicks. They follow their father around for many months, sometimes for up to a year, before they leave to start life on their own.

BIG KANGAROOS

There are many different types of kangaroo in Australia. The biggest of them is the red kangaroo, which is also the biggest marsupial in the world. It can grow to about two metres tall and lives in the drier parts of Australia in large groups called mobs. They are very strong and will kick with their big hind legs when fighting with another kangaroo, or if threatened by a human who gets too close. Although they are so large when they are mature, the baby red kangaroo is only about two centimetres long when born.

Right up until the 1900s, people advertised having large, red kangaroos as fighting attractions. The red kangaroo's habit of standing on its back legs, hitting and kicking, amused people who paid to see the spectacle of a human boxer fight with a kangaroo. Fortunately, this sad and cruel style of entertainment is frowned upon today in Australia.

EMUS

The emu is Australia's largest bird. It can grow to nearly two metres high. The male bird looks after the chicks, caring for them until they are a few months old. Once, there used to be miniature emus, but they became extinct long ago. Emus wander around looking for food and can travel over twenty kilometres in a single day. Emu eggshells were prized by some early colonists in Australia, who carved pictures on them and kept them as ornaments in their homes.

Freshwater crocodile

Baby saltwater crocodile

CROCODILES

For many years, non-Indigenous people in Australia believed in killing all crocodiles found in any settled area to keep people safe from attacks. The role of the crocodile in the ecosystem is now better known, and crocodiles are protected by legislation. Crocodiles swim up rivers and walk across the land to find their favourite habitats such as lakes and billabongs. At five metres long, a male saltwater crocodile is a ferocious creature.

Be Crocwise is a safety program run by the Northern Territory government. There are a number of safety precautions visitors must take, including avoiding the water's edge, not cooking near the water or leaving food scraps around, keeping children and pets away from the water's edge, and not going back to the same spot to collect water for camping. Crocodiles are clever. They will lie just under the water's surface, watching and waiting.

..and, of course, do not swim in water unless there is a clear sign saying it is safe and the water is croc-free.

... and the Tiny Ones

MUSKY RAT-KANGAROO

The tiniest kangaroo in Australia is only about thirty centimetres long. The musky rat-kangaroo lives in tropical rainforests, where it hops around the forest floor, looking for fallen fruit to eat. Prehistoric Australian kangaroos may have had features very like those of the musky rat-kangaroo, with its bare, skinny tail and running movements that involve using all of its four legs. Its bigger, hopping relatives live on Australia's vast savannahs and mostly use their back two legs to get around.

TINIEST POSSUM

Australia's pygmy possums are tiny. The eastern pygmy possum is only about ten centimetres long and can weigh as little as fifteen grams, causing many people to mistake it for a mouse or a baby rat. Close-up, they are delightfully cute, but also very vulnerable. Being tiny gives them little protection from predators and hiding is their only defence. Any damage to a pygmy possum's environment threatens their survival. They are not big enough to move away quickly, and can be easily caught by their predators if they are forced to leave the safety of an area they know well.

The mountain pygmy possum lives in the alpine region of southeastern Australia. It is the only Australian marsupial that hibernates. Sleeping in its nest, hidden amongst rocks, it hibernates while the snow falls through the winter, then wakes up in time to feast on the Bogong moths that emerge as the weather starts to warm up.

Land of the Marsupials

Australia has been an isolated landmass for many millions of years, giving its wildlife more than enough time to evolve into species that are unique.

Mammals are animals that are warm-blooded, have fur and produce milk to feed their babies. There are three sorts of mammals on Earth, but the marsupials are the ones that Australia can really call its own.

Where Did Dingoes Come From?

Dingoes possibly came to Australia only a few thousand years ago. They probably arrived with humans migrating from countries to the north of Australia.

PLACENTALS

These mammals include people, cats and elephants. Placentals give birth to well-developed babies. Enormous herds of placental animals live in Africa and used to dominate the landscapes of ancient Europe, Asia and America. In contrast, Australia's native placental animals are small and include only bats, rodents and dingoes.

MONOTREMES

These mammals include echidnas and platypuses. Monotremes feed their babies on milk, but lay eggs.

MARSUPIALS

Although there are some marsupials in other countries, the range of Australian marsupials is the largest in the world. They include kangaroos, koalas and wombats. Marsupials give birth to tiny babies which then usually grow inside a pouch on the outside of the mother's body.

Is It Safe to Swim?

Australians love their outdoor lifestyle. The beaches are renowned worldwide for their beauty, sparkling water and waves for surfing. Sharing the water are lots of creatures, including wonderful dolphins, fish and corals, but there could also be deadly jellyfish, sharks and crocodiles.

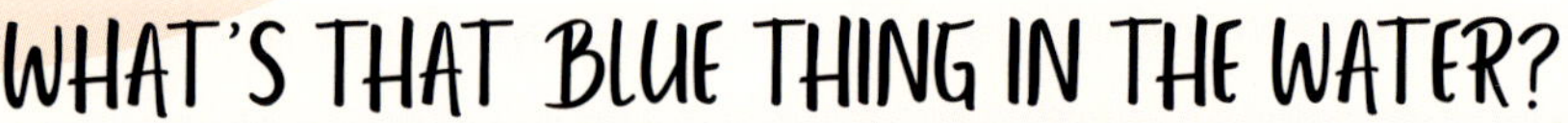

WHAT'S THAT BLUE THING IN THE WATER?

BLUE-RINGED OCTOPUS

The blue-ringed octopus is a little, brown sea creature that will suddenly flash bright blue rings or bands across its body if it senses danger. As it lives in rock pools, where children like to poke at things, the blue-ringed octopus can be a danger to them. It has strong venom which can be fatal to humans, and it bites using a beak near its mouth. This beak is so small that people may not realise they have been bitten until they start to feel sick.

BLUEBOTTLES

Beautiful blue colour, painful stinging tentacles and a weird lifestyle are three characteristics of this spectacular floating colony that often appears in the water or on the sand of Australian beaches. They are surprising creatures that look like one animal but are actually a colony of lots of little living things all joined together. Their long tentacles can wrap around people's bodies, causing rows and rows of excruciating stings. Even when bluebottles are dead and washed up on the beach, their tentacles can still cause stinging.

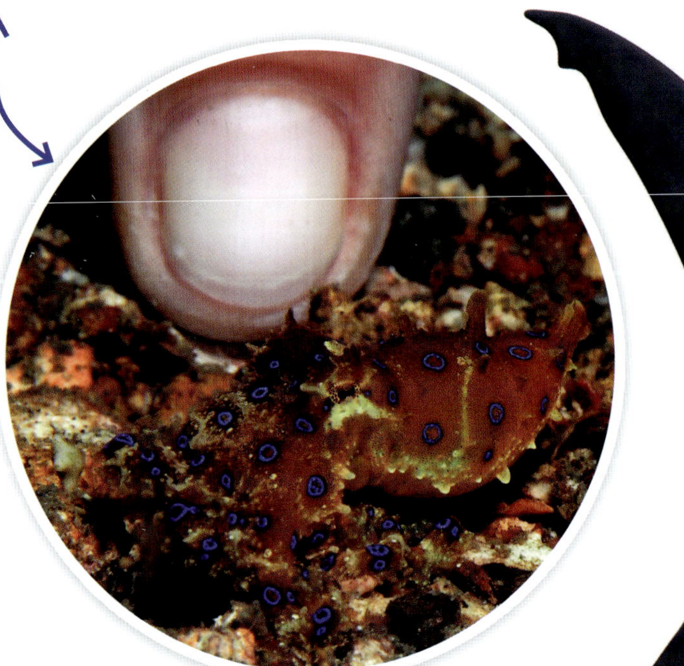

IS THAT A SHARK IN THE WATER?

Sharks and dolphins both have dorsal fins that appear above the water when they are swimming close to the surface. Dolphins are not normally aggressive, but some sharks are dangerous. So, how does a swimmer tell the difference? Shark and dolphin dorsal fins are different in shape, but trying to work out the difference is not easy when a big animal with a fin suddenly appears in the sea beside you! The safest way to swim is between the flags at a beach patrolled by lifesavers and lifeguards. They know what to look for, so you can rely on their expert experience to keep yourself safe in the surf.

Tiger shark

Bull shark

Dolphin dorsal fin

Shark dorsal fin

Dolphins like to surf, just as people do, so surfers often see dolphins beside them as they all ride the same wave together. Sharks are more interested in eating than in fun. They mistake humans in the water for seals, which are a favourite shark food.

There are three types of large shark that humans need to avoid. They are the bull shark, tiger shark and white pointer. Smaller sharks sometimes bite if they are annoyed by a human.

Dolphins may bite if a human seems to be threatening them, but they are much more likely to swim away instead.

White pointer shark

Creepy Crawlies

Blue-banded bee

When people try to think of animals that are Australian, the first ones that they add to their list are kangaroos and koalas. Creatures that are cute and furry always draw the most attention, but Australia's tiny creepy crawlies are also fascinating once you know a bit about them.

BEES THAT DON'T STING

Australia has its own native bees and one of their best features is that they are not usually aggressive and rarely sting. Some of these little bees are only five millimetres long. The native bees that form colonies are so small that, in cooler parts of Australia, they will need all the honey they produce to feed their colonies. In tropical areas, where the bees can find food all year, they produce more honey and people sometimes harvest it. This native honey has a richer flavour, ideal for honey-lovers who like to try something different.

Inside a termite mound

TERMITE HIGH-RISE

Termites are insects that eat wood. They have been guilty of destroying whole houses, where they can chew through all the wood until the house falls down. When there are no houses to eat, out in the bush, termites build their own high-rise apartments made out of mud. Often over two metres high, these termite mounds are cleverly constructed to keep the interior cool.

HAIRY CATERPILLAR TRAINS

Long lines of hairy caterpillars creeping across roads or down pathways are a feature of the Australian bush that intrigues some people and horrifies others. Travelling nose to tail, the caterpillars are out in search of food and their caterpillar trains are a form of self defence. Any predator that wants to attack them will encounter the irritating, stinging hairs of one caterpillar and then be discouraged from trying to eat the rest. When they finally end their journey, the caterpillars gather themselves into a stinging, hairy mass.

BIG STICK INSECTS

Stick insects, or phasmids, can grow to gigantic proportions. They live in forests, or in terrariums as children's pets, and can be as much as twenty-five centimetres long. Despite their size, phasmids are harmless to humans, although some have little spikes on their legs that may prick a finger. They move slowly, trying desperately to look like a twig on a tree. If really upset, the males can fly, but females stay put and rely on camouflage for protection. As well as looking like a twig or leaf, they also sway slightly, just like a branch moving in a breeze.

Camouflaged stick insect

Goliath stick insect

WITCHETTY GRUBS

These large grubs are the caterpillars of a moth that lives in Central Australia. They are a well-known bush food that is now making its way to plates in fancy restaurants. Baked and seasoned, they make an interesting meal for an adventurous gourmet. The witchetty grub is so fat because it needs to store enough energy for its adult stage, when it eats nothing because it has no mouth!

Children's stick insect

Spiders - Ouch!

Jumping spider

WARNING
Stop reading now if spiders freak you out!

There are lots of big spiders in Australia. Some of them live in the bush, while others insist on crawling around the walls inside houses.

FUNNEL WEB SPIDERS

Every year, about thirty people receive a bite from a funnel web spider in Australia. These spiders can grow up to ten centimetres in diameter, including their legs, and have venom that is delivered through large fangs.

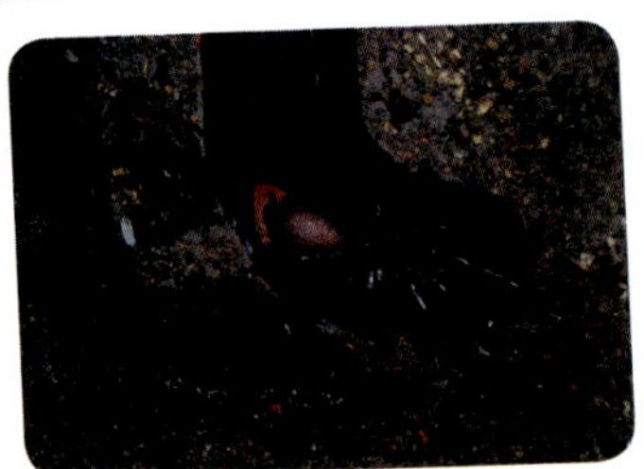
Inside funnel web nest

Funnel web nest

Close-up of Hunstman spider

HUNTSMAN SPIDERS

Huntsman spiders, often as big as a hand, seem to enjoy sitting on bedroom walls. Though they are not normally deadly, their bite is as painful as a wasp sting. Some people refuse to get rid of huntsman spiders, and happily coexist with one sitting in a corner of the ceiling. These brave people claim that their eight-legged tenants eat mosquitoes and are a great way to control annoying insects.

Animal Emblems and Symbols

All around Australia, governments have chosen animals to appear on their logos and Coats of Arms. These animals are symbolic of qualities and ideals, or they represent a particular region. The animals used as symbols are not always native Australian creatures. The lion, for example, usually represents Australia's historic ties with Britain, even though the only wild lions that lived in Britain died out in prehistoric times.

Australian Capital Territory

Faunal Emblem

Gang-gang cockatoo

Mammal Emblem

Southern brush-tailed rock wallaby

Coat of Arms of Canberra

Swans as symbols for the Aboriginal and European peoples

New South Wales

Animal Emblem

Platypus

Bird Emblem

Kookaburra

Fish Emblem

Eastern blue groper

Coat of Arms

A kangaroo represents Australia and a lion represents Britain

Northern Territory

Animal Emblem

Red kangaroo

Bird Emblem

Wedge-tailed eagle

Coat of Arms

The kangaroos hold shells found in the waters along the coast of the Northern Territory, and the eagle holds an Aboriginal Tjurunga ritual stone.

Queensland

Animal Emblem

Koala

Bird Emblem

Brolga

Aquatic Emblem

Anemone fish

Coat of Arms

Red deer - Queen Victoria gave Queensland a herd of deer
Brolga - the bird emblem
Ram's head - the sheep industry
Bull's head - the cattle industry

South Australia

Animal Emblem

Hairy-nosed wombat

Marine Emblem

Leafy seadragon

Coat of Arms

The piping shrike is a South Australian bird

Tasmania

Animal Emblem

Tasmanian devil

Coat of Arms

Two Tasmanian tigers support a shield topped by a lion. A ram on the shield represents the wool industry, and a red lion holding a pick and shovel represents mining

Victoria

Animal Emblem

Leadbeater's possum

Bird Emblem

Helmeted honeyeater

Marine Emblem

Weedy seadragon

Coat of Arms

Kangaroo holds the coronation crown

Western Australia

Animal Emblem

Numbat

Bird Emblem

Black swan

Marine Emblem

Whale shark

Coat of Arms

Kangaroos hold boomerangs, and a black swan represents the founding of the colony on the Swan River

INDIGENOUS TOTEM ANIMALS

Long before non-Indigenous people came to Australia and started choosing local animals as government symbols, the Aboriginal people had developed a totem system. A totem animal and a person share a deep spiritual connection.

But Puppies Are So Cute!

WHAT IS A FERAL ANIMAL?

Puppies certainly are cute, but not when they grow into feral dogs. Feral animals are non-native creatures that have either been released into the wild or have escaped from captivity. Once free, they increase in numbers and create havoc by destroying the ecosystem. There are feral populations of cats, dogs, camels, horses, pigs and goats all around Australia.

Rainbow lorikeet

THE DIFFERENCE BETWEEN FERALS AND PESTS

All feral animals are pests, but not all pest animals are ferals. For example, the native lorikeet is a protected bird in New South Wales, but a pest in some other states, where it feeds on crops and annoys farmers. Because it is an Australian bird, the lorikeet is not a feral animal.

Characteristics of feral animals that enable them to flourish

- They breed quickly.
- They eat a range of foods.
- They can tolerate conditions that native animals cannot.
- They have no natural predators in Australia.
- Their natural adaptability will favour them if climate change makes habitats unsuitable for native animals.

SNEAKING IN

Animals that have sneaked into Australia, usually hidden in cargo on ships or even airplanes, become pests when they escape. Mice, rats, cockroaches and fire ants are all pests that Australia wishes it did not have to deal with.

TALLY-HO

The fox is a pest that has never been a domestic animal or pet, but has been released into the bush on purpose. Early settlers released foxes and rabbits to breed and create a population of animals that people could hunt for sport, just as they used to do back home in Britain. Using trained horses and packs of hounds, and dressed in their traditional fox-hunting outfits, wealthy colonists tried hard to turn the Australian bush into a little piece of Britain downunder.

PETS OR MONSTERS?

Although cats are a great problem in the bush, where they grow to a large size and destroy wildlife, they have always been very popular as pets. In the early 1800s, cats and kittens were so valuable that they were often stolen. Ordinary cats were sold for large sums of money to colonists seeking the companionship of a little creature that reminded them of their home in Britain and that would also hunt and kill rats and mice. Australian native animals are not easily domesticated, so cats and dogs became an important commodity, and continued to be the pets of choice for the early settlers. We still love them, even though they cause so much trouble if they 'go feral'.

...AND THEN THERE'S THE CANE TOAD

It's hard to believe, but scientists actually released cane toads into Australia on purpose. The toads were supposed to eat pests that were destroying the sugar cane crop. Instead, they found other ways to spend their time, poisoning local wildlife, taking over breeding sites so that little frogs did not have a chance, and then beginning their march, or hop, across the country.

Kookaburra eating cane toad

Odd Survival Habits

If an eastern snake-necked turtle feels threatened, it can squirt a stinking liquid at its attacker from glands under its legs.

Thorny devil lizards collect water from their own bodies. Tiny grooves channel any water that falls on a thorny devil into the corners of its mouth.

The spinifex hopping mouse lives in the desert and has to conserve all of its body water. To achieve this it produces solid urine.

Water-holding frogs can live in dry deserts by bloating themselves up with water and then burrowing deep underground. They can stay there for years, waiting for rain to fall before they come back out into the open.

The stick-nest rat uses its own sticky urine to hold its nest of twigs together

Seahorses are cute, tiny fish, but the leafy seadragon is a type of seahorse that tops them all. With delicate appendages that look like floating leaves, the leafy seadragon manages to look just like

an underwater plant. This camouflage protects it from predators that would enjoy eating it.

Wombats produce poo that looks like a pile of little cubes. These poo piles are like messages to other wombats. The poo from males and females has a different smell, so wombats can use it to track down a mate.

The spotted pardalote is like a tiny, flying jewel. But this miniature bird has another claim to fame, apart from its beauty. It digs out a long and narrow tunnel in the ground and builds its nest right at the far end. This protects the nestlings from bigger birds that would attack and eat them. Pardalotes can be surprisingly bold for such tiny birds, daring to come very close to humans and even flying right inside a house if a door or window is left open.

Shield shrimps are small crustaceans whose eggs can exist in a state of suspended animation for years during long, dry seasons in the desert. When rain finally falls, the eggs hatch, filling temporary ponds with millions of shrimps. In Australia, these shrimps provide food for migratory birds that visit the wetlands created after rain falls in the desert.

Cuckoos are birds that lay their eggs in other birds' nests, then leave and take no more interest in raising their own chicks. As the large cuckoo baby grows, it takes all the food that the unsuspecting parents bring, causing the other nestlings to starve. Some cuckoo females will toss the other birds' eggs out of the nest, to make sure that their own chicks will have no competition.

You could stand near a tawny frogmouth owl for hours and never see it move. They disguise themselves as broken tree branches, sitting motionless in a tree all day.

If you look closely at an echidna's back feet, you might think it has had an injury because the feet face backwards. This is actually an adaptation to help the echidnas kick away dirt when burrowing.

When you see a kangaroo licking its arms, it is not trying to keep them clean. The kangaroo is wetting its fur so that the evaporation will help cool down its body on a hot day.

The perentie is a large desert lizard which can grow up to two metres long. With a mouth full of sharp teeth, the perentie is a meat-eating hunter. To keep its own young safe, the perentie lays its eggs inside termite hills, where the busy little termites keep the interior at just the right temperature.

Coconut crabs live on Christmas Island. They are massive arthropods, growing up to a metre wide. Like creatures out of a monster movie, these giant land crabs have a solid outer shell and huge claws to protect them from predators. Coconut crabs climb trees and also wander around on the ground searching for food. Underneath their armour plating, coconut crabs have developed a type of primitive lung that enables them to breathe on land.

The Great Barrier Reef along Queensland's coast is the only non-human, animal structure that can be seen from space. Formed by billions of tiny organisms, the coral reef has taken thousands of years to reach its current size and complexity. Coral grows just a few millimetres to a few centimetres each year.

SEE IT FROM SPACE

Finding a New Home

Migrating animals

The mighty migrations of animals across the plains of Africa dominate the subjects of wildlife documentaries. The migrations of animals in Australia are not as photogenic, but the distances travelled and the dangers overcome are just as impressive.

THE RED CRABS OF CHRISTMAS ISLAND

Every year in the wet season, starting in October, millions of little red crabs migrate across Christmas Island on their journey out of the forest down to the sea, where they breed. Even more remarkable is the fact that the miniature baby crabs make a return journey from the ocean back to the forest inland as soon as they hatch. At this stage of their lives they are only about half a centimetre long.

BOGONG MOTHS

Plain and unimpressive in appearance, the Bogong moth is a long distance traveller, making an annual round trip from Queensland or South Australia down to Victoria. Billions of them gather together in the summer and reuse the same sites every year.

MONARCH BUTTERFLY

The beautiful monarch butterfly is not a native Australian insect. People first began noticing it in the mid 1800s after it had probably been blown to Australia from nearby islands. The monarch butterflies have somehow learned to make yearly migrations between the inland and the coast, moving to areas where the weather is not too cold for them to thrive. Many of them frequently use the same resting sites, covering trees in a solid coat of orange and black butterflies.

Monarch butterfly caterpillar

Migratory birds from Asia visit the Kakadu wetlands each year. They have come on a journey that covers thousands of kilometres. Governments overseas and in Australia are anxious for these feathered travellers to be treated well, and Australia has Migratory Bird Agreements with China, Korea and Japan.

TURTLES

Marine turtles nest on Australia's Great Barrier Reef beaches. After hatching, the young turtles hurry to reach the sea before something eats them. Decades later, they return to the same beaches to lay their own eggs and continue the life cycle. During their time in the sea, the turtles travel thousands of kilometres on long migrations.

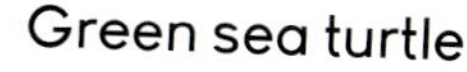

Green sea turtle

Baby turtles hurrying to the sea

Are They Real?

WATCH OUT FOR THE DROP BEARS

Tourists beware! The drop bear is a large, furry creature that will drop out of trees and attack you with its sharp claws. With the scientific name of *Thylarctos plummetus* it must be real.

But is it?

SEA MONSTERS

Stories of large sea monsters keep appearing all around Australia. Like the world famous Loch Ness Monster in Scotland, Australia's aquatic giants are very clever at avoiding people with cameras.

DEBUNKING THE MYTHS

Some of these myths were invented by people who like to make up fabulous stories, but there are also people who really believe they have seen strange and unusual creatures that no-one else believes could possibly exist. What do you think these people might have seen that made them think they have truly encountered a living monster?

LIVING DINOSAURS

So many people are obsessed with dinosaurs that they desperately want to believe that, somewhere in a hidden valley, there still might be some alive. The Burrunjor is supposed to be a large, dangerous dinosaur that is still wandering around Australia's northern deserts and savannahs.

BLACK PANTHERS

For over a hundred years, Australians all around the country have reported sightings of a creature that should not be in the Australian bush. Big, black panthers are supposed to be roaming the forests of the Blue Mountains in New South Wales, the Otway ranges in Victoria and many other remote and not so remote places. People living on the fringes of urban settlement have reported seeing black panthers near their homes as well. So, are they real? There are lots of explanations for the sightings. Perhaps people are just making up stories, or the animals might have escaped from captivity. It's a mystery waiting to be solved.

Glossary

camouflage method of hiding by disguising as something else

coexist live together peacefully

commodity something that can be traded

crustaceans crabs, prawns, shrimps and lobsters

debunk disprove

ecosystem interactions between living things and the environment

excruciating very painful

extinct animal having no living representatives

gland body part that produces useful chemicals

gourmet person who delights in the taste and creation of meals

hoax deception

megafauna very large animals from the past

oddity unusual and strange thing

savannah area of grassland plains

Top End northern parts of Australia

Index